100 FACTS
SPEED

Steve Parker

Consultant: John Farndon

Sandy Creek
NEW YORK

An Imprint of Sterling Publishing
387 Park Avenue South
New York, NY 10016

Publishing Director Belinda Gallagher
Creative Director Jo Cowan
Editorial Director Rosie McGuire
Volume Designers Dave and Angela Ball at
www.da-designs.co.uk
Cover Designer Kayleigh Allen
Image Manager Liberty Newton
Indexer Gill Lee
Production Manager Elizabeth Collins
Reprographics Stephan Davis,
Anthony Cambray, Jennifer Hunt,
Thom Allaway
Assets Lorraine King

SANDY CREEK and the distinctive Sandy Creek logo are
registered trademarks of Barnes & Noble, Inc.

© 2012 by Miles Kelly Publishing Ltd.

This 2013 edition published by Sandy Creek.

ISBN 978-1-4351-5098-0

Made with paper from a sustainable forest

Manufactured in China
Lot #:
10 9 8 7 6 5 4 3 2 1

05/13

ACKNOWLEDGMENTS

The publishers would like to thank the following artists
who have contributed to this book:

Julian Baker at J B Illustrations, Stuart Jackson-Carter,
Mike Foster at Maltings Partnership

All other artwork from the Miles Kelly Artwork Bank

The publishers would like to thank the following sources for the
use of their photographs:

t = top, b = bottom, l = left, r = right, c = center, bg = background

Cover Front: Jon Feingersh/Blend Images/Corbis; Back: (t, bg) mmaxer,
(cl) Sue Robinson, (cr) Ahmad Faizal Yahyz

Corbis 16–17 Thilo Brunner; 22(bl) PCN Photography; 26(bc) Bettmann;
36–37 Christopher Pasatieri/Reuters

Dreamstime 3(m) Joeygil

Fotolia.com 3 and 24–25(bg) Sharpshot

Getty 4–5; 10(tr); 11(br); 13 Barcroft Media; 15(tr) AFP; 17(tc) Carsten
Peter; 20–21 Dennis O'Clair; 23(b) AFP; 24(tr) AFP; 26(cl) Time & Life
Pictures; 27(b) National Geographic; 28(tr) AFP; 30–31(b)

NASA 38(br) NASA Kennedy Space Center (NASA-KSC)

Nature Picture Library 12(cl) Robin Chittenden

Photoshot 14–15 UPPA

Rex 10–11 Sipa Press; 16(bl) Ashley Cooper/SpecialistStock/
SplashdownDirect; 21(tl) Claire Leimbach/Robert Harding;
22(br) KPA/Zumas; 28–29 Charles M. Ommanney; 29(t) Curventa;
34–35(b); 38–39 Everett Collection

Shutterstock.com 1 ssguy; 6(br) papkin; 6–7 Max Earey; 7(t) JetKat;
8–9(bg) Brian Weed; 8 nuttakit; 8–9(bg) somchaij; 9(br) Picsfive;
10(bc) Garsya; 10(bl) Edgaras Kurauskas; 11(tr) piyato; 15–16(c) Ahmad
Faizal Yahya; 17(br) exclusive studio; 18–19 Kraska; 18(cl) vesna cvorovic;
19(br) Cathy Keifer; 23(t) alexkar08; 24(bl) Ralf Siemieniec; 27(tr) Graham
Bloomfield; 30(tl) Germanskydiver; 30(br) MustafaNC, Péter Gudella;
30(bl) sabri deniz kizil; 31(tl) Pavel Kapish; 31(tr) dicogm; 34(tl) Andrei
Marincas; 35(t) somchaij; 36(cl) helissente; 39(tr) bedecs

Science Photo Library 7(tr) NASA; 13(tr) David Parker; 25(br) NASA;
32–33(b) NASA; 33(cr) Peter Menzel

Topfoto.co.uk 28(bl) Topham/UPP

All other photographs are from:
digitalSTOCK, digitalvision, John Foxx, PhotoAlto,
PhotoDisc, PhotoEssentials, PhotoPro, Stockbyte

Every effort has been made to acknowledge the
source and copyright holder of each picture.
Miles Kelly Publishing apologizes for any
unintentional errors or omissions.

CONTENTS

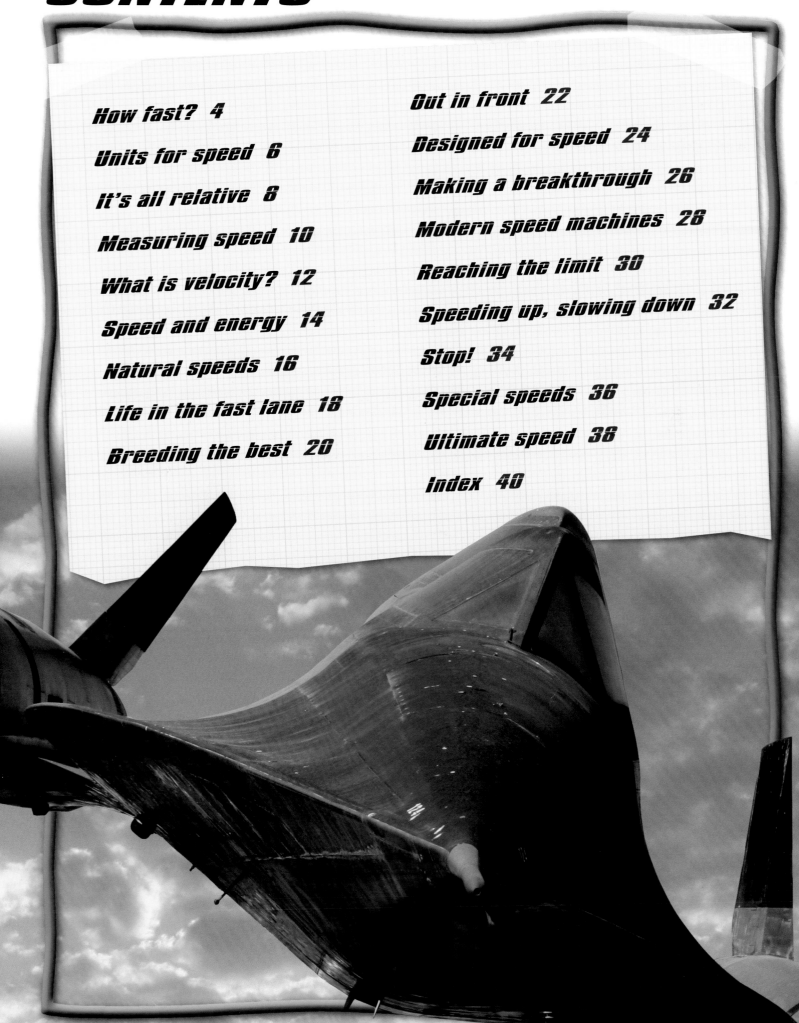

How fast?

1 Speed is how far (the distance) something goes in a certain time. If a jet plane travels 1,800 miles in three hours, its speed is 600 miles per hour. We describe speed as distance covered—such as feet or miles—in one unit or "piece" of time, such as one minute, one hour, or one year.

2 Whether something is "speedy" or fast depends on what, where, and when. Cars on a freeway travel at 70 miles per hour. A garden snail crawls along at 7 inches per minute. The snail is 10,000 times slower than the car—but speedy when compared to other kinds of snails.

3 We describe something as "high speed" if it is very fast, but what we think of as high speed has changed over time. In 1972 the fastest sailing craft was *Crossbow*, a catamaran (yacht with two hulls), at 30.2 miles per hour. Just 30 years later the record was 64 miles per hour, due to the invention of kitesurfing, in which the sailor rides a modified surfboard while holding on to a special kind of kite.

▶ Some machines are not only built for speed, they are named after it. Speedboats such as these Vee-Class powerboats go faster than 100 miles per hour, their super-streamlined hulls slicing across the wave tops.

Units for speed

4 Speed is the distance covered in a set time. A racing car might have a speed of 100 miles per hour for one lap of its course, but it might go at 185 miles per hour on straights and 30 miles per hour around bends. The 100 miles per hour is the average speed—total distance divided by total time.

$$SPEED = \frac{DISTANCE}{TIME}$$

6 The knot is used to measure how fast something goes on water. Its name comes from the fact that ships used to measure their speed by letting a rope out into the water. The rope had knots at regular intervals and a float at one end. The more knots that passed over the ship's side in 30 seconds, the faster the speed. One knot is equal to 15 miles per hour.

Knots

▶ Sailing speeds are still often measured in knots— as are wind speeds.

5 Throughout history, people have measured distance, time, and speed in lots of different ways. Long ago, the time for a journey by sailing ship was measured to the nearest day, or even the nearest week! Today, modern jet planes mean the journeys are measured in miles or kilometres per hour.

Miles
per hour
(mph)

▶ The speed indicator dial on fast cars may go up to 200 miles per hour.

Feet
per
minute

▶ For a snail or a slug, 3 feet is a very long distance.

7 Even today there are many different ways to describe speed around the world. In most of Europe, road speed is measured in kilometers per hour (km/h). In the UK and U.S. it is measured in miles per hour (mph).

Feet per second

▲ Comets travel through space at more than 220,000 feet per second, but seen from Earth, they appear to be hardly moving.

▶ Most passenger jet planes have a cruising speed of around 560–590 miles per hour.

Miles per hour (mph)

8 To describe and imagine very fast or slow speeds, we have to change the measuring units we use. A rocket must reach more than 25,000 miles per hour to blast away from Earth into space. This is known as escape velocity. It may be easier to imagine as 7 miles per second, or even 37,000 feet per second.

9 Special units can help us when comparing speeds. A cheetah is much faster than a cockroach, but this is mainly because it is much bigger. However, if we compare each animal's speed to its size, things are rather different. A cockroach covers 50 of its own body lengths per second, but the cheetah covers just 12 of its own body lengths per second.

10 All speeds are relative. This is because nothing in the Universe is completely still. Even someone measuring speed is moving! So you can only measure something's speed "relative" to something else—that is, by how fast it goes past.

11 A single object has many different speeds. A train goes at 60 miles per hour relative to its tracks and stations. For a person in a car traveling alongside the track at 40 miles per hour, the train's speed is 25 miles per hour. For a passenger on a train traveling toward the first train at 60 miles per hour, the combined speed is 120 miles per hour.

① To a person standing still at a station, the passing train's speed would be 60 miles per hour.

② For a driver in a car traveling alongside the train, its relative speed is 25 miles per hour.

③ For passengers in an oncoming second train, the combined speed is 120 miles per hour.

12 Usually we measure speed as the distance traveled here on Earth, along the surface or through the air—but this is also relative. The Earth's surface is moving as the planet spins once each day. If you could stay put in space, high above the Earth, someone standing still at the Equator (an imaginary line drawn around the midpoint of the Earth) would be moving at 1,516 feet each second.

▼ ② The Equator is the fastest-moving place on Earth, being the widest part, in the middle of the direction of spin.

EQUATOR

◄ ① This person is standing still at the Equator. But is he moving? Not relative to the Earth's surface. But if seen from space, then yes—as fast as a jet fighter plane.

13 As well as constantly spinning, the Earth travels on its yearly orbit around the Sun. This makes working out speed even more complicated, since Earth's average orbital speed is about 19 miles each second.

▼ ③ Like the other planets, Earth zooms at huge speed around the Sun.

▲ ④ The Sun and millions of other stars are flying in space at gigantic speed, as the whole Galaxy swirls around.

14 Added to this is the speed of the whole Solar System (the Sun and all its planets). It is whirling around the center of our massive group of stars, the Milky Way Galaxy. This speed is even faster—about 150 miles each second.

15 Even if you went into deepest space, there is still nowhere that you can stand to measure "true" speed. All the galaxies are flying away from each other, some at more than 186 miles per second. The whole Universe is moving faster and getting bigger.

Measuring speed

16 Long ago, there were no standard ways of measuring speed because there was no accurate way to measure time. People used devices such as sand clocks (in which sand poured through a small hole) to measure time, and methods such as counting their own steps to measure distance. The only way of comparing the speed of two or more things, such as horses, was a head-to-head race.

▼ The Olympics showcase the world's fastest humans in direct competition. Here Vomma Iso-Hollo wins 1932's 3,000 meters steeplechase.

17 Gradually, measuring devices became more accurate. The first stopwatch was developed in the 1850s, and by the 1910s it was accurate to 1/100th of one second. During the 1970s, digital stopwatches increased this to 1/1,000th of one second.

▼ Stopwatches used clockwork springs and measured to 1/100th of one second. Electronic timing devices use vibrating crystals to measure to 1/1,000th of one second.

18 To measure distance, people once used lengths of wood. This gave rise to units of length such as the pole or rod, equivalent to 16.5 feet. Tape measures arrived in the 1700s, and by 1970 laser beams could measure distances more accurately.

▲ A race result may be so close the human eye cannot see who has won. A photo finish uses a sequence of pictures, 1,000 or more each second, to pick out the winner, as in this 100-meters sprint.

19

For distance and speed over long distances, such as across seas, people relied on maps and charts. They measured the distance on the map and multiplied it by the scale of the map. But this was not very accurate—a very thin line on the map could be many hundreds of feet wide in the real world.

20

From the 1990s the "satnav" system GPS (which stands for Global Positioning System) meant speed over long distances could be measured much more precisely. GPS satellite clocks are accurate to 14 billionths of one second, and the best GPS receivers can pinpoint position to within 10 inches.

Each satellite transmits its identity and position

Some satellites are farther away, so signals arrive at the GPS unit at different times

GPS unit in vehicle is "tuned in" to the signals from the satellites

▲ A "satnav" receiver compares the times taken for signals to arrive from at least three GPS satellites.

21

Some sports have special ways to measure speed. The Hawk-Eye system uses several video cameras to record a ball's path from different angles. A computer compares the pictures and calculates the ball's speed and direction. A fast baseball pitch is 100 miles per hour, and a tennis serve can be 150 miles per hour—220 feet in one second!

▼ In tennis, the Hawk-Eye tracking system shows the ball's speed, position, and direction, and also if it landed on, in, or outside the line.

OFFICIAL REVIEW

What is velocity?

22 Speed is distance covered with time—but it has no direction. To describe speed in a certain direction, we use the term "velocity." A swan might have a speed of 40 miles per hour when it migrates to its breeding area, but its velocity is 40 miles per hour due north.

23 Measuring velocity means measuring time and distance (as for speed), and also position. For long distances this can be done using GPS or "satnav" equipment. In smaller areas it can be done with a map, perhaps using local landmarks, or with short-range radio signals such as radio beacons used by aircraft.

◄ This gray reef shark's radio tracker gives its position at different times, showing its overall velocity on longer journeys between reefs, and how, for example, ocean currents affect its movements.

24 Velocity gives much more information than speed. It shows changes in speed, direction, and location, and how fast and how often they happen. This helps aircraft pilots to work out the fuel needed to climb to cruising height, go around storms, and circle or "stack" waiting to land.

► As the plane passes through each criss-cross radio "grid," the pilots work out its velocity to land safely.

Time taken between grids gives speed

Grid of radio signals

The plane's location in each grid gives its position

▲ When the smallest particles of matter are smashed together, they go on amazingly complicated curved pathways or tracks. These show their size, speed, and structure.

25 On the huge scale of space travel, knowing about speed and direction, and so velocity, is vital. As a space probe sets off for a distant planet it must aim exactly in the right direction. Otherwise, after a journey of perhaps ten years, it could be millions of miles off course. Space scientists continually check its path to keep it on target.

26 On the tiniest scale, velocity helps us to understand the world of atoms and their parts. These particles are smashed together with incredible force, such as in the world's largest machine, the LHC (Large Hadron Collider). The velocity of the resulting bits—their speed and direction—gives clues to their most basic makeup.

◀ An Air Force jet fighter watches space shuttle *Atlantis* on its final blastoff in 2011. The jet plane is capable of 1,600 miles per hour. As the shuttle docks with the orbiting International Space Station, both the shuttle and the station will be traveling ten times faster. And both in the same direction—and so with the same velocity.

QUIZ

1. Rather than heading north, then the same distance east, what would be a quicker direction?

2. What is the name of the world's largest machine?

3. What is wrong with saying "The car's velocity was 70 miles per hour?"

Answers:
1. Head northeast
2. Large Hadron Collider
3. You need to give the car's direction as well as its speed

Speed and energy

27 Something that moves has not only speed, but also a form of energy—the ability to cause changes and make things happen. Energy due to movement or motion is called kinetic energy. You can see it at work everywhere—it is used to generate electricity from rushing river water and it is the reason that we have airbags and seatbelts in our cars.

29 Massively heavy things are more difficult to speed up. They have high inertia, which means they need lots of energy to give them motion. The heavy flywheel in an engine needs great force to get it going, but once it's spinning, it helps the engine run smoothly.

▶ One very strong human—Mikhail Sidorychev—can gradually overcome the inertia of a huge plane, giving it kinetic energy to get it moving.

28 Kinetic energy depends on two main features—an object's speed, and its mass (amount of matter). The faster something goes, the more kinetic energy it has, and the more mass it has, the more kinetic energy it has. So a very fast motorbike could have the same kinetic energy as a very slow truck.

HOW FAR?

You will need:

tennis ball   stiff card about 24 inches long
pen   measuring tape

1. Draw a scale on the card, marking every one inch. Prop up one end of the card at an angle of about 30° to make a ramp.
2. Release the ball from each mark in turn. Measure how far it rolls each time. The ball gains more speed from each higher mark, and so has more energy to roll farther.

30
Once an object is moving with speed, it has lots of kinetic energy, or high momentum. Then it resists losing speed—being slowed down. A huge, speedy ship such as an oil tanker has so much momentum that it may take 30 miles to slow down.

▼ On a "Wall of Death," fast-circling riders produce enough outward force to overcome gravity and rise at right angles up the wall.

▼ Racing bikers have to learn how to slow down and lean into corners.

31
As an object goes around a bend or curve, it has different forces acting on it, and this affects its speed. A motorcycle can go fast in a straight line, but around a bend it must slow down as the rider leans to one side so that its tires don't lose grip and skid.

32
Spinning at speed causes another set of forces. One is felt as a pull away from the center of the spin. This is known as centrifugal force, and is used in machines called centrifuges. A medical centrifuge spins tubes of blood so fast, the heaviest parts sink to the bottom of the tube. This helps to separate blood into its different parts.

Natural speeds

33 The natural world has a huge range of speeds, from incredibly slow to ultra-fast. Some of the slowest movers are the world's landmasses or continents. They drift around the planet's surface by a few inches each year.

34 Glaciers are thick "rivers" of snow and ice. They slide downhill, mostly by a few feet each year. In Greenland, the Jakobshavn Glacier sped along at more than 7.5 miles per year, probably due to global warming.

35 Rivers have many different speeds, from 32-plus feet per second down steep rapids to less than 3 feet per minute in other places. The giant Amazon River's average flow speed is about 1.2 miles per hour. One of the fastest ocean currents is the Agulhas Current in the Indian Ocean, at 6.2 miles per hour.

▼ Where a river flows through a narrow gorge, it speeds up as rapids. The same amount of water passes every second as in places where the river is less restricted.

32 ft/second

7.5 mi/year

▼ A scientist using an instrument called a theodolite. This records the exact position of marker poles at certain times to determine a glacier's speed.

36 In 1980, the eruption of Mount St. Helens, in Washington State, caused an avalanche and rockfall that traveled at more than 250 miles per hour. This was one of the fastest ever measured. Even a small avalanche can reach 75 miles per hour, which is much too fast to outrun.

400 km/hour

▼ "Storm-chasers" follow storms, partly for thrills. Many will record a storm's track. Here a storm-chaser drops a weather probe (red) in the path of an oncoming tornado.

38 Violent winds such as hurricanes and tornadoes can reach speeds of more than 250 miles per hour. Even faster, at 430 miles per hour, is a pyroclastic flow—a cloudlike surge of superheated gas and rock particles from a volcano. The tsunami wave from an underwater earthquake goes even faster in the open ocean, up to 620 miles per hour.

700 km/hour

QUIZ

1. What is a theodolite?

2. Which volcanic eruption in 1980 was one of the fastest ever measured?

3. What is the top speed of a tsunami wave?

Answers:
1. An instrument used to measure the speed of a glacier
2. Mount St. Helens
3. 620 miles per hour

Pyroclastic flow

▶ Pyroclastic flows can pick up even more speed as they spread down steep hills under the pull of gravity.

37 The speed of sound in air varies with air's temperature and pressure. Near the ground it has an average speed of 767 miles per hour, or around 1,115 feet per second. So the boom from a thunderstorm 3 miles away takes 14 seconds to arrive.

Life in the fast lane

39 An animal's speed depends on the environment in which it is moving. The sailfish cuts through water at 70 miles per hour. The cheetah sprints on land at about the same speed. The peregrine falcon is the fastest of all animals—its stoop or "power dive" through the air can reach speeds of over 185 miles per hour.

185 mph

Part-folded wings lower air resistance

40 Cheetahs are famously fleet-footed, but there are lots of other speedy creatures. The fastest reptile is the spiny-tailed iguana lizard, which runs at 22 miles per hour. The speediest shark—the short-fin mako—swims at more than 40 miles per hour, while the fastest mammal swimmer is the killer whale or orca at 35–plus miles per hour.

Small head for streamlining

Flexible backbone

70 mph

Tail works as an air rudder to change direction

Powerful muscles in shoulders and hips

▲ The cheetah's long, slim, flexible body and long legs allow it to cover 26 feet in each bound.

41 Animal adaptations for speed on land include long legs for lengthy strides, and powerful muscles in the shoulders and hips. In water, fast fish such as marlin have stiff, crescent-shaped tails that they thrash from side to side so fast, they look like they are quivering.

Stiff, narrow, curved tail

42 One of the fastest muscle actions in the animal world is the mantis shrimp's clublike pincer or claw. It "locks" in a bent position using a triggerlike part, builds up muscle force, and then "unlocks" to throw a punch that lasts less than 1/200th of a second, moves at 72 feet per second, and strikes with the force of a rifle bullet.

◄ The peregrine does not simply fall downward in its stoop. It flaps its wings for even greater speed.

Wing feathers fanned for greater push

43 Inside living things, one of the fastest actions is the movement of nerve signals. They can travel at more than 330 feet per second, going from human toe to brain in less than 1/50th of one second.

44 Plants can be speedy too. The venus flytrap flicks its leaf shut around an insect victim in less than half a second. Plants such as giant kelp seaweed and some types of bamboo grow at great speed—up to 3 feet each day.

70 mph

Top (dorsal) fin folds down at speed

Pointed snout for less water resistance

▲ Blocks of powerful muscles along the sides of the sailfish's body swish its tail from side to side, and make up more than three quarters of the fish's weight.

▶ If this fly touches the trigger hairs near the hinge of the venus flytrap's leaf, the trap at once snaps shut.

19

Breeding the best

45 People have held races to find the speediest animals and people for more than 5,000 years. Early races involved horses, camels, dogs, and humans. Running and chariot racing were among the most popular events at ancient Greece's Olympic Games, 2,500 years ago.

47 People can select the fastest animals of each kind, and breed them together to produce even speedier ones. This process is called selective breeding. It has produced the fastest type of dog, the greyhound. It races at almost 66 feet per second (45 miles per hour)—nearly twice as fast as a human sprinter.

Long muzzle

Small ears

Slender, athletic body

Muscle bulk in shoulders and hips

Long tail has a fine point

Thin but strong legs

▶ The greyhound's speedy features have been selected since the 1700s.

46 Some of the biggest prizes are given for the fastest racehorses. Perhaps the quickest was Secretariat, an American thoroughbred that raced in the 1970s. He set records that still stand today, winning the 1973 Kentucky Derby at 55 feet per second (37 miles per hour).

▼ Fast-action photos show how a racehorse's leg-moving muscles are concentrated in the shoulder and buttock areas. Most of the leg is slim and easy to swing fast.

▲ The fastest camels are almost as rapid as racehorses, reaching speeds of over 35 miles per hour.

50 Training a champion animal speedster is a complicated business. Trainers pay great attention to diet and exercise, working out a series of activities that build gradually to the day of the big race. Some racehorses only run well if they have their "best friend" stable companion with them on the day—which might be a donkey!

48 Many animals are raced for speed and stamina (endurance). Strange races include camels, ferrets, maggots, elephants, sled–pulling husky dogs, hamsters in wheeled cars, and pigs with pretend stuffed–toy "jockeys." Elephants weigh over 5.5 tons yet they can reach speeds of 22 feet per second (15 miles per hour).

49 Breeders look for several features in racing animals. These include a slim but muscular build, strong bones (especially in the legs), no spare fat, a strong heartbeat, and clear breathing to take in the oxygen in air needed by hardworking muscles.

WORM OLYMPICS
You will need:
earthworms   A4 paper
sticky tape

1. Roll and tape sheets of A4 paper into tubes about half an inch wide.
2. Tape the paper rolls side by side.
3. Carefully gather garden earthworms and put each one into a tube at the "Start" end.
4. The worm that is first to emerge completely at the "Finish" end is the winner!

Note: After your race, put the worms back in the soil where you found them and wash your hands.

Out in front

51 Human speeds improve year by year. In 1912 the record time for the 100 meters sprint was 10.6 seconds. Today it is more than one second less. This is partly because people have generally become healthier, with better food and fewer illnesses, especially in childhood. We also understand more about exercise and how the body works.

53 Human speeds have also increased for money reasons. Modern sport is big business that attracts the best brains to train athletes. Coaches devise incredibly detailed training programs covering everything from building muscle and improving breathing, to planning their athlete's mental approach to each race.

Strong bone structure

Efficient lungs and heart

Slim arms

Narrow hips and slim legs

Minimal body fat

▶ From 2008, Jamaica's Usain Bolt shattered sprint records and became World and Olympic champion at 100 and 200 meters, at speeds of up to 37.5 kilometers per hour.

Powerful pump-action arms

Tall stature

Muscle bulk in hips and legs

Long legs for extended stride

52 Some people have innate (inbuilt) features, which help them to run fast. Being tall and muscular with long legs is ideal for short-distance sprinting. A smaller, slimmer, lighter build is more suited to long distances.

◀ Britain's Paula Radcliffe has the narrow, lightweight shape of a long-distance runner. She took the world marathon record in 2003 at an average speed of 11.6 miles per hour.

54 Every so often, a great landmark is reached in human speed. In 1954 English runner Roger Bannister was the first person to run a mile in less than four minutes—which many people said was impossible. In 1968 Jim Hines of the U.S. broke the "10-second barrier" and ran the 100 meters sprint in 9.9 seconds.

▶ When Bannister broke the four-minute mile, people doubted the time could reduce much more. Today's runners are 15 seconds faster.

▼ In 100 years, the record time for the 100 meters freestyle swim—here with modern French champion Alain Bernard—has reduced from 66 to 46 seconds.

55 There are lots of different human speed records. These range from the 60-meter "flying start" and sprints at 100, 200, and 400 meters, to middle-distance 800 and 1,500 meters, and long-distance 5,000 and the marathon (26.2 miles). If sprint swimmers in a 50 meters front crawl race could maintain their speed over 1,500 meters, they would cut the record time for that race (currently 14 minutes and 30 seconds) by four minutes!

Designed for speed

56 The quest for speed has led people to design, build, and operate all kinds of speed machines. From soapbox carts and penny-farthing bicycles to racing cars, powerboats, jet trucks, bullet trains, and rocket planes—as with human speed, machine speed keeps improving through the years.

Contoured helmet

Arms and hands together

Slippery body suit fabric

Spokeless disk wheels

▲ Track cyclists use every design trick to reduce air resistance or drag.

57 One important feature of a speed machine is its overall size. Bigger is usually faster, but only up to a certain point. A larger machine can have a bigger, more powerful engine, but the weight of the machine itself, with its frame and working parts, increases greatly and speed becomes slower again.

Mirrors close to body

Bonnet "flows" into windshield

▶ Air is pushed over a car smoothly, rather than being allowed to go underneath and lift it at high speed.

Low sloping front

Rounded front wheel arches

◀ A hydrofoil lifts up at speed to reduce drag on its hull.

58 "Drag" is the enemy of speed. Drag is the resistance or pushing-back force from air or water, as an object shoves between its tiny particles or molecules. A speed machine is shaped to be streamlined or "slippery" with a pointed front, smooth surfaces and curves, a tapering rear end, and no sticking-out parts.

59 Before building a speed machine, design models can be tested in wind tunnels or water tanks. This shows how the air or water flows past the vehicle. It reveals any swirls, eddies (circular movements), or vortexes (unsteady movements), which may increase drag and have a slowing effect.

Gradual rear slope

Rear wing presses down back wheels for better grip

Minimal airflow under car

60 Speed machines cannot be totally smooth and streamlined, because they need to move in a steady, stable, safe way. So they may have ridges, fins, or wings that act like wings in reverse, pushing the car's wheels down onto the ground for extra traction (grip).

61 Computers also help to design speed machines. A virtual design, existing only in the computer, can be put into a virtual wind tunnel or water tank, also in the computer, to see how it performs. By pressing a few keys the designers can redesign a part to try and improve performance.

▶ Computer modeling shows how swirling air currents are "thrown off" the rear parts of a fast plane, slowing it down.

Making a breakthrough

62 Through history, different types of speed machines have got faster by small amounts. A big leap in performance is usually the result of a new invention or development, such as a new engine, better materials that save weight, or a new control method, such as a computer.

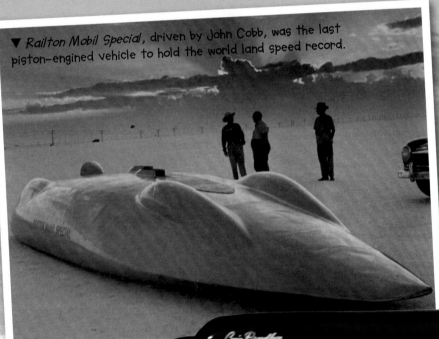

▼ *Railton Mobil Special*, driven by John Cobb, was the last piston-engined vehicle to hold the world land speed record.

63 In the early 1950s a new kind of propeller-driven speedboat made a huge splash. *Slo-Mo-Shun IV* used a method called prop-riding, where the boat's hull rose at speed to lift the top parts of the propellers above the surface. This reduced their pushing force but reduced drag even more. It improved the water speed record by 37 miles per hour in two years, to 178 miles per hour.

▼ *Spirit of America* became the first jet car to take the land speed record, powered by an old GE J47 engine from a Saber jet fighter plane.

64 In the late 1940s the world land speed record was held by John Cobb in *Railton Mobil Special*, at 394 miles per hour. This vehicle had piston engines that turned the wheels, like an ordinary car. By 1965 the record had shot up to almost 620 miles per hour with Craig Breedlove in *Spirit of America*, due to the arrival of the jet engine.

FASTEST OR FARTHEST?

You will need:
computer   printer   A4 paper

1. Go to www.factsforprojects.com and click on the paper planes link.
2. Make two planes—the Condor is like Concorde and the Bullet is like the X-15.
3. Test them outdoors on a calm day. The dart goes fastest, but the glider may stay up longer and fly a greater distance. It's not always fastest that goes farthest.

65 In 1938 the steam locomotive *Mallard* set the speed record for railed vehicles, at 125.9 miles per hour. Then along came electric trains, which soon pushed the record higher, and by 2007 it was over 350 miles per hour. Maglev trains, which "float" above rails, go even faster.

Front view of train

Track levitation magnet

Close up

Section through rail

Train levitation magnet

Train guide magnet

▲ Maglev trains use magnetic levitation—magnetic forces that suspend the train over the track, removing the problem of wheels and friction.

▲ Concorde was the fastest-ever passenger aircraft. But fuel costs, noise, and old age led to it being retired in 2003.

67 The invention of the jet engine had a huge effect on aircraft speed records. The fastest propeller plane was probably the Russian Tu-114 passenger aircraft of the 1960s, at 540 miles per hour. By 1969 jet-powered Concorde had more than doubled this to 1,349 miles per hour. Today jet fighters reach over 2,000 miles per hour.

66 The fastest of all powered machines have rocket engines. In 1967 the U.S.'s X-15 rocket plane reached 4,519 miles per hour, which is still a record for any manned vehicle or craft—apart from in space. Returning from the Moon in 1969, Apollo astronauts reached 25,000 miles per hour.

▲ The X-15 was launched in mid air from a giant bomber aircraft. Two X-15 flights zoomed for a few seconds to the edge of space, over 60 miles high.

Modern speed machines

68 Apart from kitesurfers and windsurfers, the fastest sailing craft is *Hydroptère*. It has one main hull and two smaller outer hulls, and is a hydrofoil, rising up at speed on winglike struts. The craft took the record in 2009 with a speed of 60.8 miles per hour.

69 In 1997 the UK's jet car *Thrust SSC* roared across Black Rock Desert to set the land speed record of 763 miles per hour. It was driven by fighter pilot Andy Green, with former record-holder Richard Noble as team boss. "SSC" stands for Super-Sonic Car, because the vehicle also broke the sound barrier as it set the record.

▲ *Hydroptère* made several failed attempts on the water speed record—during one of which it almost sank—before its 2009 success.

▲ *Thrust SSC* caused a sonic boom as it scorched across Nevada's Black Rock Desert, on its record-breaking two-way run.

70 In 1978 the world water speed record of 317.6 miles per hour was set by Ken Warby in his homemade, jet-powered craft, *Spirit of Australia*. It was on Bowering Dam, Australia, with perfect conditions of wind and water surface. This record is one of the most dangerous, and two attempts to break it have killed the pilots. Warby's record still stands.

▲ Warby built *Spirit of Australia* in his garage, using a secondhand jet engine given by air force friends.

71 To design, build, test, and run a new record-breaking speed machine costs huge amounts of money. This is one reason why main speed record attempts are rare. Teams hoping to take the land speed record include the North American Eagle Project, the UK's *Bloodhound*, and Australia's *Invader 5R*.

Jet engine air intake

▶ *Bloodhound* aims to attempt the land speed record by 2015, depending on how much money is raised.

Stabilizer wing

Nose wheel

Pointed nose

72 Apart from trains specially altered to break records, there are also records for the fastest regular or scheduled railway service. In 2011 a new type of train—called a "bullet train" because of its shape and speed—linked the Chinese cities of Beijing and Shanghai. It carries 500 people and can reach 300 miles per hour.

73 To get away from the vast cost of breaking the all-out best speed, there is increasing interest in human-powered craft and vehicles. There are records in the air, on land, and water, and even underwater. The human-powered submarine *Omer 5* set the underwater record in 2007, at 9.3 miles per hour.

Reaching the limit

74 Speeds cannot keep increasing forever. To break the land speed record, *Thrust SSC* needed an incredibly flat surface and a straight course of almost 13 miles. Faster cars will probably need longer courses, until the Earth's landscape is the limit.

◀ Skydivers move their arms, legs, and body position to speed up or slow down. The belly-to-earth position gives a fall speed of 118 miles per hour.

75 As an object goes faster, the opposing drag or resistance rises too, at an ever-increasing rate. Eventually, resistance equals forward force, and the speed limit (terminal velocity) is reached. As parachutists free-fall to Earth, they are pulled by gravity but slowed by air resistance. When these forces balance the parachutist has terminal velocity, which is about 125 miles per hour.

76 Speeds are limited for safety reasons. On roads in built-up areas, speed limits are usually around 30 miles per hour. Accident information shows that at this speed, about one person in ten hit by a car dies. At just 10 miles per hour more, nine in ten die.

▼ Stopping distance increases in proportion. At 60 miles per hour, it is over three times more than 30 miles per hour, not twice.

SPEED	THINKING DISTANCE	BRAKING DISTANCE	STOPPING DISTANCE
20 mph	20 feet	20 feet	40 feet
30 mph	30 feet	45 feet	75 feet
40 mph	40 feet	80 feet	120 feet
50 mph	50 feet	125 feet	175 feet
60 mph	60 feet	180 feet	240 feet
70 mph	70 feet	245 feet	315 feet

◀ A car's rev counter warns of danger above 7,000 rpm. This is when the engine is turning more than 115 times each second.

77 Engines, motors, and other machines have speed limits for their moving parts. Otherwise damage is likely as parts spin or move so fast that they crack and shatter. Many cars have a dial showing engine rpm—revolutions (turns) per minute. The high end of the dial is colored to warn against making the engine turn so fast.

▼ Formula I car engines turn at up to 18,000 rpm. At this speed, if one tiny engine part fails, the whole engine may shatter and catch fire.

78 Computers may seem the fastest machines, but even they have their limits. They work by moving particles called electrons, which are pieces of atoms, in the form of tiny pulses of electricity. But electrons need energy to push them along, and they have a maximum travel speed. The upper limit may be reached in 15–20 years.

ROLLER SLIDE RACES

You will need:
children's play slide   string
pair of roller skates
objects of different weights

1. Choose two items of different weights and tie one to each skate.
2. Let both skates go from the top of the slide at the same time. Note which one reaches the bottom first.
3. Repeat for several objects. Does the heaviest one always win?

Speeding up, slowing down

79 Hardly anything goes at a steady speed—not even planets traveling around the Sun. The Earth's speed varies by more than 2,200 miles per hour between the fastest and slowest part of its orbit. Movement always involves speeding up, called acceleration, and slowing down, or deceleration.

▼ Top Fuel dragsters are the fastest-accelerating cars. From standstill, they cover a one-quarter-mile track in five seconds, finishing at a top speed of over 310 miles per hour.

80 The rate of change for speed is measured by how the distance covered in a certain time changes with time. A car starts from standstill, goes 3 feet per second after one second, 6 feet per second after two seconds, and so on. Its rate of acceleration, or speeding up, is 3 feet per second per second. This is usually written as ft/s^2.

▲ This car speeds up from standstill to 60 miles per hour in ten seconds. So its average rate of acceleration is 6 miles per second per second, or 6 miles/sec^2.

81 Speeding up and slowing down are caused by a change in force, such as an engine turning faster or wind blowing harder. A familiar example is when something falls to Earth's surface under the force of gravity. In theory, this causes an acceleration of 9.81 m/s^2, often known as the "g force." In reality, air resistance reduces this acceleration.

▶ Lieutenant Colonel John Paul Stapp experiences extreme g forces during a rocket-propelled acceleration and deceleration exercise in which he reached 632 miles per hour in five seconds.

At standstill

Early acceleration

82 Bigger planets than Earth have much stronger forces of gravity, so their g forces are higher. On the largest planet, Jupiter, falling objects would accelerate at 82 ft/s^2. On the Moon, which is much smaller, this would be 5.2 ft/s^2.

83 Accelerometers measure how fast things speed up or slow down. Most contain small crystal-like parts that change shape slightly as their rate of movement alters, producing tiny amounts of electricity. Two of these devices at right angles can track the direction of a movement, as well as acceleration.

▲ If a micro-accelerometer (seen on the hand at the front of the image) detects a car's sudden slowdown, the safety airbag inflates in one tenth of one second.

84 Accelerometers are used in hundreds of everyday objects, from airbags in cars to the handheld controllers for computer games and cell phones. They are also used to detect motion in volcanoes and cliffs that might warn of eruptions, earthquakes, and rockfalls.

Greatest acceleration

Top speed

Beginning to decelerate

Greatest deceleration

Stop!

85 What speeds up, eventually slows down. Less speed, or deceleration, is a vital part of working machines, motors, and engines. To save time and stay safe, many of them have specially designed ways of slowing down.

86 Some kinds of brakes use drag or resistance. Fast planes have air brakes—flaps on the wings or body that fold out into the passing air to increase drag. Very fast planes release a parachute at the rear when they need to slow down fast, for example when landing on an aircraft carrier.

▶ On a short runway, the F-117 Nighthawk stealth fighter uses a parachute as an air brake, to help it slow down when landing. This saves wear on the wheels, tires, and brakes.

87 Brakes are a common way to slow down. Most use rubbing or friction, which converts kinetic energy (the energy of movement) into heat energy. Many cars have disk brakes, in which stationary pads on the car rub against a disk attached to the road wheel. In many types of electric saw the spinning blade is "grabbed" by a friction device to slow it down fast when the motor is switched off.

Brake lever

Brake pad presses on disk

Steel brake disk

Piston

Brake pipe

Disk rotates with wheel

◀◀ Hydraulic fluid pushes a piston that presses the brake pad against the turning brake disk on a motorcycle wheel.

88 If the driver of a speeding car brakes too hard, the wheels may lock and skid, so the vehicle goes out of control. A car's ABS (anti-lock braking system) senses this and makes the brakes "pulse" on and off many times each second, under computer control. This prevents wheel lock and slows the car more safely.

Full-face helmet

Mesh across the window prevents the driver's arm from going through the window in the event of a crash

Sides of seat curve around the driver's ribcage while straps keep him or her securely in position

Flameproof suit

Roll cage made from steel tubing

▲ Each NASCAR stock car racer has more than 30 safety changes, or modifications, from the standard or "stock" version for that model of car.

89 Slowing down too fast can be harmful and even deadly. To protect people inside, vehicle makers design crumple zones to soak up the energy, rigid bars or cages around the driver, and passenger areas, airbags, seat belts, head restraints, and other safety devices.

QUIZ

1. Which of these will help a car to brake—an airbag, a disk brake, or a turbocharger?

2. What do brakes convert kinetic energy into?

3. What does "ABS" stand for?

Answers:
1. Disk brake 2. Heat energy 3. Anti-lock braking system

Special speeds

90 Speed crops up where many people would not think about it. These special uses and examples of speed range from making music to catching people who are driving over the speed limit, to predicting the weather.

91 Fast aircraft may measure their speed in Mach numbers. These compare the speed of an object to the speed of sound under the same conditions of air temperature and pressure. The speed of sound is always Mach 1. An aircraft flying at Mach 0.9 is traveling at nine tenths of the speed of sound. At sea level this is about 690 miles per hour. Very high, in cold thin air, it is 618 miles per hour.

▶ A shock wave of air (area of very high pressure) forming around this F-18 Super Hornet shows it is close to going faster than sound.

92 Speed is part of how things vibrate, or move to and fro. This is known as frequency, measured in Hertz (Hz). Twenty Hz is 20 vibrations per second, the lowest or deepest sound human ears detect. A piano's highest or top note is 4,186 Hz.

▼ High-pitched or high-frequency sounds have shorter waves than low or deep ones.

High pitch (short wave)

Low pitch (long wave)

0 Calm Chimney smoke rises straight up

1 Light air Smoke drifts gently

3 Gentle breeze Washing flutters

2 Light breeze Leaves rustle

4 Moderate breeze Paper blows around

7 Near gale Whole trees start to sway

5 Fresh breeze Small trees sway

9 Severe gale Small branches, tiles, and chimneys blown off

▼ The Beaufort Scale does not measure the actual speed of the wind in miles per hour or knots, but what the wind does to its surroundings.

11 Severe storm Serious damage

6 Strong breeze Hard to control an umbrella

8 Gale Difficult to walk into wind

10 Storm Houses damaged; trees blown down

12 Hurricane Widespread damage

93 The Beaufort Scale for wind speed goes from 1, no wind, to 12, hurricane, and describes the wind's effects. For example, at 4 on the scale, dust and loose paper are raised and blown about, and small branches begin to move.

95 The speed of the shock or seismic waves from an earthquake or volcano shows its strength and how far damage will spread. These waves travel at 2–4 miles per second through rocks near the Earth's surface, but much faster—over 7 miles per second—through the middle of the planet.

94 "Speed guns" that check vehicle speeds use a feature of speed called the Doppler effect. The gun beams pulses of radio or similar waves and detects them as they bounce back off the vehicle. The faster the vehicle, the more it moves toward the gun between pulses, so the closer the bounced-back pulses are.

I DON'T BELIEVE IT!

Tornadoes on Earth have wind speeds of over 215 miles per hour. On the planet Neptune, storm winds blow over six times faster, at 1,370 miles per hour!

96 Modern science tells us that the fastest possible speed is the speed of light. It is about 186,410 miles per second. This means light could go around the Earth seven times in less than a second. As far as we know, nothing can travel faster.

97 The speed of light is usually written as the symbol c. It is so important that it is the only speed that is fixed or constant, everywhere at any time. In fact, it is more constant than time itself. Scientists explain weird events in deep space by saying that time can go faster or slower, but the speed of light cannot.

▼ The fastest-ever human-made objects, capable of reaching 157,078 miles per hour, were two *Helios* spacecraft sent to study the Sun in 1974.

QUIZ

1. Which are faster—radio waves, microwaves, or X-rays?

2. Does light go slowest in space, air, or water?

3. How many days in a light year?

Answers:
1. They all travel at the speed of light. 2. In water 3. A light year measures distance, not time.

98 Light speed is not only for light waves. It is for all similar kinds of waves, known as electromagnetic waves. These include radio waves, microwaves, infrared and ultraviolet rays, X-rays, and gamma rays. Also the speed of light is usually measured in a vacuum (a space empty of matter). It is slightly slower in air, and even slower in water.

▲ Like all forms of light, laser light beams—such as those seen here at a concert—go as fast as radio, X-rays, and all other waves made of electrical and magnetic energy.

99 Will it ever be possible to exceed light speed? Some experts suggest ideas such as "warp drive." Instead of light passing through space, space is bent or warped to pass around the light beam.

100 Going faster than the speed of light would lead to many strange events. One idea is that as you approach light speed, time slows down. At light speed, time stops. So faster than light could allow you to travel back in time. Then you could read this book all over again and be just as amazed!

▲ In science fiction on TV and in movies, craft such as Star Trek's *Enterprise* sometimes go faster than light—perhaps when being pulled into a massive black hole.

index